11 July   With Rose de Roscoff onions, an early maturing and delicious variety

No dig, a simple and easy method

METHOD

1 Soil is undisturbed, its organisms can work and multiply. You build on the existing network of life.

2 Organisms are fed with organic matter on the surface, as in nature but faster. This is because decomposition has already happened in heaps, together with a multiplication of microbes.

Adding compost / decomposed materials enables soil organisms to work their magic more quickly.

3 Plant feeding is about biology (fungi etc.) more than chemistry (nutrients / minerals).

No dig increases the ability of plants to find food which is already there.

RESULTS

1 Speed

For example, you can plant into a new bed created on weeds, on the same day, even with perennial weeds still alive underneath.

Fast turnover in summer from easy bed preparation: clear remains of first harvest and quickly pop in plants for autumn and winter harvests

2 Ease

Weeds appear less, since their healing properties are not needed by healthy soil.

Soil does not stick to your boots.

You can walk on your beds, thanks to soil's firm but open structure.

3 Productivity

No dig uses less compost than an equivalent area dug, because from cultivation, and active soil life increases fertility.

Reduced need to weed makes closer spacings more practical.

Jack Wallington, garden columnist of *The Daily Telegraph* and garden designer,
**I was reading Mary Keen's piece this morning myself with interest.
right, that you've managed to convert almost the entire gardening world to no dig.**

January 2021

Your beds are ready for spring if you spread compost last year. Otherwise spread compost now, on the surface where soil organisms like to feed. Do not 'fork in' any organic matter, just let nature take care of it. Think in terms of feeding soil life generally, rather than feeding specific plants. In damp climates, compost is better than straw for giving minimum habitat to slugs.

If you still have a mass of weeds to clear, mulch either by covering with cardboard (and compost above it), or polythene (with compost below it).

Excluding light from weeds makes them grow futile leaves in darkness. This slowly starves their roots, until they die in situ and without any cultivation or removal. Meanwhile the compost is feeding soil life and gives your plantings a fast start.

In January, I advise you sow no seeds because they will struggle to grow in the cool and darkness, then would be overtaken by later sowings. Ignore any seed packet advice to sow in January!

24 January   A cornucopia of January vegetables, some stored and some freshly harvested, lambs' lettuce at top

A winter frost and view of mostly empty beds, tall plants are broccoli for spring harvests

Monday	Tuesday	Wednesday	Thursday	Friday	Saturday	Sunday
				1 No sowing, and a great month for preparing beds and paths, even for occasional weeding if weather is mild	**2**	**3**
4	**5**	**6**	**7**	**8**	**9**	**10**
11	**12**	**13** ● New moon	**14**	**15**	**16**	**17**
18	**19**	**20**	**21**	**22**	**23**	**24**
25	**26**	**27**	**28** ○ Old / Wolf full moon, 19.18 GMT	**29**	**30**	**31**

February 2021

From mid-February, when daylight suddenly increases, you can make first sowings under cover.

This is earlier than seeds would germinate naturally, hence the need for extra warmth, for example in your house. Most seeds do not need light to germinate, just warmth.

Germination needs higher temperatures than actual growth. Even place trays in a warm cupboard for a few days until you see emerging leaves. Or buy an electric propagator. At Homeacres we make a hotbed of fresh horse manure.

26 February   Seedlings in the unheated greenhouse from sowings 7–15 February, and they germinated in my conservatory for 5–7 days before moving here

In cooler climates, make these first sowings in early March. If using the warmth of your house, I recommend setting up some LED grow lights, to have sturdy rather than leggy seedlings.

My sowing dates are based on the time of year above all, and moon phases to a lesser degree. They suggest a general time of first sowing, and many vegetables can be sown again later. Find extra sowing and job timings in my Diary, and more about no dig in my new no dig book.

11 February   Salad boxes in the unheated greenhouse after four picks so far, growing in Morland Gold organic potting compost with no feeding

Monday	Tuesday	Wednesday	Thursday	Friday	Saturday	Sunday
1	2	3	4	5	6	7
8	9	10	11 ● New moon	12	13	14 St Valentine's Day — Same sowings as 15 & 16
15 ∧ Spring onion, lettuce, spinach, coriander, early cabbage, broccoli, broad beans, peas for shoots, coriander, parsley	16 ∧ Aubergine, peppers, chillies	17	18	19 ∧ Onion, radish, kohlrabi, beetroot	20	21
22	23	24 ∧ Onion, spring onion, lettuce, spinach, coriander, early cabbage, broccoli, broad beans, peas for shoots, coriander, parsley	25	26 ∧ Early peas	27 ○ Snow full moon 08.19 GMT	28

March 2021

Early spring means dealing with new weeds emerging, at tiny seedling stage. It's quick to either hoe or rake lightly on a dry day, or hand weed if moist and if weeds are larger. With a hoe or rake you can be rid of a lot of weeds very quickly, before any sowing and planting. It's called a 'weed strike'.

Tiny weeds are easily killed by their roots being disturbed. At the same time your hoe or rake is breaking a few lumps, making an even surface for sowing and planting.

2 March   Charles dibbing holes to transplant multi-sown radish, peas already transplanted from sowing three weeks earlier, bed then covered with fleece

Early weed strikes mean that summer in the no dig garden sees much less weeding needed.

If the weather is warming by mid-March, you can make outdoor sowings of cold-hardy vegetables such as lettuce, carrot, parsnip, spinach, onions, peas and broad beans. However, if your beds have many weed seeds, either wait until after hoeing them, so that crop seedlings are not smothered by weeds, or raise plants under cover so that you can easily hoe the outdoor weed seedlings before planting.

18 March   Eating now at Homeacres, March vegetables from store and freshly picked, the squash is Crown Prince

Monday	Tuesday	Wednesday	Thursday	Friday	Saturday	Sunday
1 ☼ Garlic if not already sown ∧ Beetroot, onions, radish, turnips	**2**	**3**	**4** ∧ Peas for shoots, spring onion, lettuce, spinach, coriander, parsley, early cabbage, broccoli, broad beans, pepper, aubergine, chilli	**5**	**6** ☼ or ∧ Peas and broad beans	**7**
8 Same sowings as 6 & 7	**9**	**10**	**11**	**12**	**13** ● New moon ☼ or ∧ Lettuce, spinach, coriander, parsley, early cabbage, calabrese, peas for shoots	**14**
15 Same sowings as 13 & 14	**16** ☼ or ∧ Broad beans, peas ∧ Tomatoes, aubergine, peppers, chillies, peas for pods	**17**	**18** ☼ Parsnips, onion seeds and sets, turnips, radish ∧ Celery, celeriac, beetroot	**19**	**20**	**21**
22	**23**	**24** Lettuce, spinach, spring onions, early cabbage	**25** Top day for catch up sowings	**26** ☼ or ∧ Peas for pods, ∧ Tomatoes	**27**	**28** ○ Worm / Sap full moon, 19.50 GMT ☼ Parsnips, carrots, first early potatoes, onion sets ∧ Celeriac
29 Same sowings as 28	**30**	**31**				

April 2021

Finally it's time to sow many warmth-loving and frost tender vegetables, but not outside unless your climate is warm. There is no rush because later sowings grow more strongly and may overtake earlier sowings. Sow tomatoes as late as early April. From mid-April, sow courgettes, squash and sweetcorn.

Wait until May before sowing summer beans under cover, and tender plants outside.

Sow potatoes now: first earlies straight away, second earlies and maincrops around mid-month.

Sow peas and broad beans if you have not already.

Reduce slug habitat, especially close to new sowings and plantings. Mow grass short, avoid planting close to stone walls and overhanging shrubs, and keep the garden tidy. Mulch with compost rather than straw or undecomposed mulches, which give moist shelter to slugs. You actually want the surface to dry sometimes. An exception is summers of hot sun, when it helps to mulch with undecomposed materials such as grass and old leaves.

22 April   Before the first pick of pak choi, rocket, spinach and Gem lettuce sown in early February; already flea beetle holes on pak choi and rocket

7 April   This largest head of purple sprouting broccoli weighs 680 g / 1 lb 9 oz, then smaller shoots grow after it is cut

Monday	Tuesday	Wednesday	Thursday	Friday	Saturday	Sunday
			1 ∧ Basil, celery, leeks, leaf beet	**2**	**3** ∧ Tomatoes to grow outside, soybeans	**4**
5 ✻ Carrots, parsnips, beetroot, early potatoes	**6**	**7**	**8**	**9**	**10**	**11**
12 ● New moon	**13** ∧ Courgette, squash, pumpkin, sweetcorn, soybeans	**14**	**15** ✻ Second early & main crop potatoes	**16**	**17** ∧ Frost-tender flowers: marigolds, zinnias, cosmos etc.	**18**
19	**20** ✻ Leeks, spring onions, chard, leaf beet	**21**	**22** ∧ Courgette, squash, pumpkin, sweetcorn, soybeans ∧ Cucumber to grow under cover	**23**	**24** ✻ Carrots, beetroot, and potatoes if not already sown, also top days for catch up sowings	**25**
26	**27** ○ Pink full moon, 04.33 GMT	**28** ✻ or ∧ Chard	**29**	**30** ∧ Courgette, squash, pumpkin, sweetcorn ∧ Cucumber & melon to grow under cover		

May 2021

Sowings in May define your summer and autumn harvests, even winter ones. For example the first half of May is good for under cover sowings of summer beans, autumn cabbage and Brussels sprouts. Brussels are not easy to grow well, and I suggest F1 varieties for tight buttons.

Basil and beans need steady warmth to grow. Even in mid-May, best results are from germinating seeds under cover, to avoid damage from cold nights and winds. Plus this reduces losses of precious seed from pests such as slugs.

Spring is the season for aphids, hatching out from winter hibernation. May is awkward because aphid numbers have to increase, before predators can get going themselves. I find that watering is the best way to reduce damage, because aphids like dry conditions and plants stressed by lack of moisture. Water leaves where the aphids are clustering, and roots so that plant strength increases.

Check the date of your likely last frost. At Homeacres for example it's mid-May, so I transplant nothing frost-tender before that.

10 May   Three-strip trial with overwintered broad beans, broccoli (transplanted seven weeks earlier) and potatoes on right

16 May   Edward planting cucumbers, just after last frost, four-week-old plants

Saturday	Sunday	Monday	Tuesday	Wednesday	Thursday	Friday
1 ∧ Courgette, squash, sweetcorn First week remove fleece covers in Zone 8	**2** Maincrop potatoes if not already	**3**	**4**	**5** Spring onion, autumn cabbage, Brussels sprouts	**6**	**7**
8	**9**	**10**	**11** ● New moon	**12**	**13**	**14**
15	**16** ∧ Spring onion, autumn cabbage, Brussels sprouts, celery second sowing	**17**	**18**	**19** ∧ & ☀ if warm, sweetcorn, courgette, squash, pumpkin ∧ French beans, climbing beans	**20**	**21**
22	**23** Top day for catch up sowing	**24** Basil	**25**	**26** ○ Flower full moon, 12.15 GMT	**27**	**28** French and climbing beans, ∧ Cucumbers for outside
29	**30** Swede, rutabaga	**31**				

Sowings are ☀ unless marked ∧

June 2021

Be among your plants as much as possible through summer, when growth is so rapid, including those few weeds. Keep pulling new shoots of perennial weeds such as bindweed and marestail.

There are joyful first harvests of summer's finest: peas, broad beans, early potatoes, carrots, beetroot and broccoli. Meanwhile you can sow winter vegetables in modules, so that seedlings start growing while the early harvests are finishing.

Multi-sow beetroot to transplant at 35 cm / 14 in apart, for harvest through autumn and for winter storage. Transplant the leeks you sowed in April, and the brassicas you sowed in May.

2 June   A morning's harvest of calabrese Green Magic F1, cabbage Cape Horn F1, carrots Nantes Milan with beetroot Boltardy, salad leaves, and broad beans Aquadulce Claudia sown in November

Swedes grow large as singles for winter use, transplanted at a month old. Raise under cover (greenhouse or polytunnel) to keep seedlings free of flea beetles, which can decimate outdoor sowings of all brassicas until late summer. Cover new brassica transplants with mesh.

Sow carrots in drills 30 cm / 12 in apart. Water these before you sow, so that moisture is right beside and below the seeds.

After mid-month, harvest softneck garlic before the tops go yellow, then hardneck garlic in early July. Prune trees of stone fruits such as plums.

Evening view from house after a very dry May and some welcome rain

Monday	Tuesday	Wednesday	Thursday	Friday	Saturday	Sunday
	1	2	3 Lettuce for summer, kale	4	5	6 Carrots, beetroot, swedes
7 Same sowings as 6	8	9	10 ● New moon	11	12	13 Same sowings as 14 & 15
14 Winter cabbage, romanesco, broccoli, kale, first chicory for hearts	15	16 Dwarf and climbing beans	17	18 Carrots, beetroot	19	20
21	22 All seeds esp. winter cabbage, romanesco, broccoli, kale, dwarf beans	23	24 ○ Strawberry full moon, 19.40 GMT	25	26 Carrots, beetroot	27
28	29	30 Last sowing of basil				

Sowings are ✲ unless marked ∧

July 2021

Sowing times become more precise from now, with shortening days ahead. A useful rule of thumb is that every growing day in July is equivalent to two in August and a week in October.

In early July sow chicories to form bittersweet radicchio hearts in autumn, and savoy cabbages for hearts in late winter, plus there is still time to sow kale, and carrots for small roots. In late July, sow bulb fennel and Chinese cabbage for autumn harvest, coriander and chervil for picking through autumn, winter and even spring.

2 July Evening view, almost every bed is full because we make new plantings as soon as harvests finish, for example of peas and broad beans at this time of year

Continue your habit of regularly pulling weed seedlings – quick, easy and more enjoyable than being overwhelmed by large weeds. If there are many weed seedlings, hoeing is quicker.

Second early potatoes are often fully grown by mid-July: harvest asap in order to plant leeks or brassicas, including kale and broccoli. In rainy weather check for late blight on potatoes and harvest as soon as you see any damage.

Until mid-July is good for summer pruning of apple trees, and remove any fruits that now look crowded.

6 July Rose de Roscoff just pulled, to dry 2 weeks in open

Monday	Tuesday	Wednesday	Thursday	Friday	Saturday	Sunday
			1 Chicories and endives	**2**	**3** In warm climates, last sowings of dwarf beans	**4**
5 Sowings are ☼ unless marked ∧	**6** Kohlrabi, last sowings of beetroot, carrots	**7**	**8**	**9**	**10** ● New moon	**11** Frizzy & scarole endive, lettuce for autumn, chicories, chard, kale, kaibroc/brokali, chard for autumn into spring
12 Same sowings as 11	**13**	**14**	**15**	**16**	**17** Wallflowers & Sweet William (*Dianthus*) for flowers next spring	**18**
19	**20**	**21**	**22**	**23** Florence fennel, last kohlrabi	**24** ○ Thunder full moon, 03.37 GMT	**25**
26	**27**	**28** Last lettuce for autumn, endives, Chinese cabbage, kale, land cress, coriander, dill, chervil	**29**	**30**	**31**	

August 2021

Give most water to plants in full fruit, such as cucumber, beans and tomatoes. Give less to winter vegetables which are not swelling as much now.

Early August is fantastic for sowing salad rocket, pak choi and other oriental leaves, for harvests through autumn and perhaps into early spring. August's first half is optimum for sowing spinach, the prince of vegetables, which has passed its flowering time and crops for seven months when sown now.

Land cress sown early August often survives winter and crops until flowering next May. The leaves taste of iron, and steel you for cold weather!

Around 10 August, pinch out the tops of cordon tomatoes and continue to remove side-shoots. This diverts energy into existing fruits, rather than new trusses which would not have time to ripen before mid-October.

In late August, sow spring onions and spring cabbage to overwinter as small plants. Then they bulk up next spring, when you will be so glad you remembered to sow them now.

9 August   With new planting of broccoli under mesh, lettuce just picked and gladioli flowers this end, most beds have second plantings

16 August   Greenhouse harvest 8.3 kg beef tomatoes, 3.7 kg aubergines; one week since the previous harvest

Saturday	Sunday	Monday	Tuesday	Wednesday	Thursday	Friday
	1	**2**	**3** Winter radish of many kinds, including mooli	**4**	**5**	**6**
7 Spinach, salad rocket, mustards, pak choi, tatsoi, land cress, coriander, dill, chervil	**8** ● New moon	**9**	**10** Spinach, and pinch out tomato tops	**11** Turnips, winter radish	**12**	**13**
14 *Phacelia* for May flowering	**15**	**16** Spinach, salad rocket, mustards, pak choi, chervil	**17**	**18**	**19** Turnips, winter radish	**20**
21	**22** ○ Grain full moon, 13.02 GMT	**23**	**24** Spinach & salads for winter outside inc. Claytonia (winter purslane) and mizuna. Onion seeds for June harvests	**25**	**26**	**27**
28	**29**	**30**	**31** Kale & chard to transplant under cover; spring onions, spring cabbage, Claytonia, mizuna to transplant outside			

Sowings are ❊ unless marked ▲

September 2021

September's first half is the best time to sow salad plants, chard and kale. Transplant them under cover in October when tomatoes and summer crops finish. These are for small but frequent harvests through winter.

- Multi-sow three seeds per module and thin to two plants for rocket, mustards, spinach and claytonia.
- Or sow in trays to prick out, for example lettuce and endive which are easier to harvest from single plants.

8 September   I do mixed plantings to maintain diversity and to look beautiful, in blocks and/or beds so that harvests and pest protection are easier

There is still just time to sow spring cabbage and White Lisbon spring onion, which can be harvested at all stages of growth next spring. From late May, leave a few spring onions to grow into white bulbs in early summer, when onions are scarce. White Lisbon does not attract mildew, so is an alternative to planting sets in October.

Cabbages develop hearts at different times: if you have a lot to eat at any stage, make sauerkraut. Some hearts stand until November, then store in a cool shed.

With the year's fourth compost heap, its front unscrewed to show contents

Monday	Tuesday	Wednesday	Thursday	Friday	Saturday	Sunday
		1	**2**	**3**	**4** ∧ Kale & chard both to transplant under cover ∧ Spring onions, spring cabbage, lambs lettuce, wild rocket to transplant outside	**5**
6 ● New moon	**7**	**8**	**9**	**10**	**11**	**12** ∧ Lettuce, spinach, any salads and herbs to transplant under cover; spring onions to transplant outside or under cover
13 Same sowings as 12	**14**	**15**	**16** Florence fennel to grow under cover, bulbs late winter	**17**	**18** White mustard for green manure in any beds empty until early spring	**19** Last ∧ sowings of brassica salads for winter under cover, rocket, mustards, mizuna Claytonia, lambs' lettuce
20 Same sowings as 19	**21** ○ Harvest full moon, 02.58 GMT	**22**	**23**	**24**	**25**	**26** Garlic
27 Garlic	**28**	**29**	**30**			

Sowings are ✳ unless marked ∧

October 2021

Carrot harvests are exciting, you never know for sure what is there and they smell gorgeous. I advise pulling sooner rather than later, before slugs and root flies become too interested. Whereas celeriac and beetroot add weight in October and are best left to grow.

Sow cloves of garlic now, preferably and cheaply those of your finest bulbs, or some store-bought, organic garlic. There are two types: hardneck gives flower stalks you can eat in May as 'snapes', and large cloves which are easy to peel, while softneck garlic grows larger bulbs without scapes.

Spreading homemade compost after clearing dwarf beans and planting garlic, for June harvest

Autumn is time to feed the soil: after clearing any weeds, spread compost to nourish soil life and thus plants throughout the coming year.

Mulch your beds with a compost layer of 3–5 cm / 1–2 in, to cover the surface completely. If it's lumpy, use a fork to break into small pieces before spreading, then frosts will break the lumps further. If weeds are thick, lay cardboard before spreading compost.

16 October   New interplanting of lambs' lettuce between swedes

Monday	Tuesday	Wednesday	Thursday	Friday	Saturday	Sunday
				1	2	3
4	5	6 ● New moon ✷ Garlic	7	8	9	10
11	12	13	14 ✷ Garlic	15	16	17
18	19	20 ○ Hunters' full moon, 15.58 GMT	21	22	23	24
25	26	27	28	29	30 ✷ Broad beans, garlic if not already	31

November 2021

The absolute best sowing in November is broad beans, Aquadulce Claudia, for early harvests next spring. Even here where winters are mild, I find best results from sowing by mid-November, preferably under cover and with a mousetrap nearby.

Vegetable gardens' ornamental qualities offer glowing contrasts to November gloom. There is strong colour in leaves of red cabbage, chicories, chard and beetroot. I love the sculptural qualities of sharp-edged leek leaves, sprawling broccoli, asparagus ferns as they turn golden, and globes of celeriac doing a final swell.

19 November   Charles spreading compost wherever beds become empty after final harvests

November offers wonderful harvests: cabbage hearts, root crops, kale, leeks, even spinach if you sowed it in August.

Salads still crop outside in mild areas, such as rocket, mustards, endive, radicchio, lambs' lettuce, land cress and winter purslane. Pickings of new leaves are smaller as daylight declines, but are larger under cover. Grow some plants in a box of compost, on staging in a greenhouse. Pick a few leaves all through the milder spells of winter.

28 November   The day's harvests include chervil, spinach, celeriac, leeks, Oxhella carrots and celery

Monday	Tuesday	Wednesday	Thursday	Friday	Saturday	Sunday
1	2	3	4 ● New moon	5	6	7 — Same sowings as 8 & 9
8 ∧ or ❋ Broad bean	9	10	11	12	13	14
15	16 ∧ Broad bean and last garlic	17	18	19 ○ Frost full moon, 09.00 GMT	20	21
22	23	24	25	26	27	28
29	30					

December 2021

Frosty morning sunrise when the atmospheric pressure was a record 1050 mb

No dig offers many advantages, and reducing slug numbers is a big one in damp climates. I had often wondered why I was relatively untroubled by slugs, and at a conference in Norway one indication came from Professor Elaine Ingham, soil microbiologist from Oregon. Her work shows how soil cultivation causes mini layers of compaction, resulting in anaerobic fermentations producing alcohol, which slugs enjoy.

No dig keeps carbon in soil rather than losing it to air as CO_2, or having it eaten by oxygen-stimulated microbes after digging. Increase your soil carbon by spreading a mulch of compost to feed worms and other valuable organisms, plus feed soil life in paths with some woody wastes or rough compost. The excretions of soil organisms provide food for your plantings through all of next year, because their nutrients are not water soluble.

The biggest timesaver follows as soil stays calm and less weedy, with its weed seeds undisturbed.

I wish you readers, and your worms, a joyful festive season!

Garden view with Jack Dowding's No Dig sign from scrap metal

Monday	Tuesday	Wednesday	Thursday	Friday	Saturday	Sunday
		1	2	3	4 ● New moon	5
6	7	8	9	10	11	12
13	14	15	16	17	18	19 ○ Cold full moon, 04.38 GMT
20	21	22	23	24	25	26
27	28	29	30	31		

Latest harvest July 2020. From homesaved garlic seed, my original seed was eating garlic from a greengrocer 22 years earlier

Glossary

Annual
Growth starts from seed and finishes within a year

Bed
An area for vegetables and flowers, may or may not be raised, and with no dig is often mulched / covered with compost

Cardboard
Brown not shiny, usually corrugated, and tape or staples removed before use

Compost
Decomposed organic matter, usually dark and crumbly but often not of even consistency. Old animal and human manure is compost and often lumpy. Other composts include leaf mould, wood chips and bark, potting composts, plus what you make at home, and the two below

Digging
Soil broken by spade or fork to say 25 cm / 10 in depth, with compost usually buried, also called 'incorporated'

Drill
A channel 2–3 cm / 1 in deep for sowing seeds, made by rake, hoe or finger

Firm
A natural condition of soil, neither compacted nor loose or fluffy

Green waste
Proprietary compost made from garden wastes, also 'municipal'

Manure
Animal poo with variable amounts of bedding, decomposed for garden use

Microbes
Mostly beneficial and invisible soil organisms such as bacteria, fungi and protozoa

Mulch
Surface material, either to exclude light and retain moisture, or to feed soil organisms, or both

Mushroom compost
'Waste' product from growing mushrooms in a proprietary compost

No dig
Soil is not disturbed, while its inhabitants are fed with organic matter on the surface

Nutrients
Food for plants, also called minerals in the USA

Path
Access strip between and around beds

Perennial
Growth continues every year from an established network of roots

Planting
Plants going into holes made quickly by a dibber, more slowly by a trowel

Sides
Optional edging for beds, often made of wood, or edges can simply slope

Soil
Earth surface which plants root into, the lower levels are subsoil

Sowing
Seeds going into drills/holes made in a compost mulch, or in propagation trays

Under cover
Sheltered from weather by polythene or glass, with sufficient light for growth

Charles in a nice breeze doing the second winnow of land cress seed and pods in July, from overwintered plants

Seeds and varieties

VARIABLE GERMINATION

Every year I suffer poor germination from one or more company's seed, easily confirmed as I often sow two different lots of the same vegetable at the same time. Comparing germination reveals the poor ones, often a result of the seed being old.

Should this happen, I suggest you send an email. Officially they will assure you that germination tests showed a good percentage success. However, this is commonly in perfect laboratory conditions!

HYBRIDS OR OPEN-POLLINATED SEED?

'Open-pollinated' (or OP) means natural breeding has happened to produce that variety of vegetable, and you can save seeds from it. Breeders need to maintain these OP varieties by selection of harvests. This apparently earns less money than breeding F1 hybrids and, perhaps because of that, the maintenance of OP characteristics sometimes slips.

- Gardeners' Delight tomato in the 1980s was a small, sweet cherry, whereas many 'Gardeners' Delight' seeds now grow larger and less sweet fruit. The seed packet has the same name, but results are different.

- The words 'heirloom' and 'heritage' mean only that a variety originated x years ago, and does not guarantee quality, or even flavour sometimes.

A FEW OF MY SELECTIONS

Beetroot Boltardy has good flavour and grows well in all seasons except winter. I have been successful with early Boltardy since 1983, but recently the roots have been less round and dark. For later sowings from mid-April, sow Boldor and Touchstone Gold for a lovely flavour and yellow colour; Chioggia gives pretty pink and white stripes when cut, while Cheltenham Green Top is long and sweet, and stands well in winter.

Broad bean For sowing in autumn to overwinter, Aquadulce Claudia is reliable and develops great flavour if beans are allowed to mature until white and creamy. It also crops well from sowing by early March. Masterpiece Green Longpod has tasty green beans, and Green Windsor has arguably the best flavour of all.

De Monica grows a smaller plant of 1.2 m / 4 ft high, with pods of 4–5 pale-coloured, sweet beans. Robin Hood is similarly small.

Broccoli A common broccoli in climates with mild winters is Purple Sprouting to overwinter, and sowing in June is good for this. I grew Early Purple Sprouting for many years, with fair results. Then I tried Claret F1 and have not looked back – large main heads in April, followed by many secondary broccoli shoots, finishing

Garlic Once you have a harvest of bulbs that you like, I recommend keeping the largest bulbs to separate into cloves to re-plant in early October. Hardneck varieties make slightly smaller bulbs, harvest about two weeks later than softneck varieties, and are easier to peel when cooking.

Onion Onion fly is increasing and mildew has become more common, so I am growing onions from seed to avoid risk of contamination from sets. Sturon is good for long storage, Stuttgarter has strong flavour and a flat shape, Rose de Roscoff matures early and yields highly. Long Red Florence is mild and does not keep beyond Christmas. For mildew resistance try yellow skinned Santero which stores well too. For spring onions, my favourite continues to be White Lisbon. And Lilija grows nice red spring onions, as well as bulbs.

Potato First earlies in order of maturity: Swift, Rocket, Dunluce and Casablanca. Second earlies: Charlotte, Apache, Estima, Wilja, Vivaldi and Ratte (salad). Maincrop: Sarpo varieties for blight resistance, King Edward.

Spinach Spinach for both cooking and salad can be had from October to May from Medania sown in August outside, or early September to grow under cover. Sow Medania and F1 varieties in March, to crop by May for six weeks: harvest by pinching off larger leaves. To have green leaves through summer it is more reliable to grow leaf beet or Swiss chard.

Tomato Sungold orange cherry has a fine, refreshing sweetness and ripens early. Sakura F1, a red cherry, offers great flavour and larger fruits. Matina, Orkada F1 and Ace give red, medium-size fruits. Marmande is ever-reliable for beef tomatoes, Black Russian/Krim are great for tasty dark fruit, Feo de Rio is excellent for beef tomatoes, and the Brandywines for top flavour. All do best under cover in most of Britain, unless it is a hot summer. For outdoor tomatoes in temperate climates, try Crimson Crush F1 for juicy flavour and blight resistance.

Winter squash Red (or Uchiki) Kuri gives red fruits of excellent flavour, which manage to ripen in damp summers. Crown Prince's blue-grey fruits are of superb taste and sweetness, ripening a month after kuri. Butternut's tasty fruits are slow to ripen unless summer is hot: their skins need to be brown and hard, for best flavour and to store through winter.

---

by mid- to end-May. Try also Kaibroc and Brokali, for small plants which are very fast at heading into small spears. Sow as late as mid-July, for cropping in October onwards, even into winter.

Brussels sprouts Fresh, well-grown Brussels actually have lovely flavour, with less bitterness than in bought buttons. Doric F1 has always grown well for me as a late cropper from December to March, while Marte F1 is excellent for cropping from September to December. Groningen is a tall, open-pollinated variety. Flower Sprouts (F1 hybrid cross with kale) have open buttons of sweeter flavour and are less prone to caterpillars.

Cabbage For autumn cabbage try Piacenza and Quintal d'Alsace from Real Seeds, while Filderkraut makes large, pointed hearts which are tender and delicious in coleslaw or for sauerkraut. In November 2019, I harvested hearts of 4–5 kg (60 cm / 24 in spacing) and they were so sweet.

For red cabbage I like Rodynda and Granat. They both keep for 2–3 months in the shed, from a harvest in late autumn.

For early cabbage sow Cape Horn F1 before the end of March. While savoy cabbage can be sown June and planted in July, to harvest in late winter when greens are so welcome. Savoy hearts are frost hardy.

Carrot Early Nantes, for early and later sowings, grow vigorously to a fair size, with good sweetness. Berlicum and Autumn King varieties are good for sowing by mid-June, to store through winter. Coloured varieties have variable vigour: yellow ones grow easily, purple ones are more tricky, all have different flavours.

For winter harvests of great flavour and storing quality, try the stump rooted Oxhella, best sown in June.

Cucumber Outdoor cucumbers need no training and grow easily when it's warm outside! Ma Diva and Tanya cucumbers are prickly like most outdoor ('ridge') cucumbers – just peel the skin before eating. Home grown are tasty, you should notice a big difference compared to what you can buy.

All-female cordon cucumbers for growing under cover are expensive seed, and highly productive. I like Carmen F1 for whole-size fruits and Passandra F1 for half-size cucumbers, and I grow them up strings.

French bean Climbing beans come in many shapes and colours. Blauhilde has lovely purple pods, Fortex (Seaspring Seeds) has surprisingly long ones of good flavour, and Cobra is a green all rounder and crops all summer, really nice beans.

My favourite dwarf beans are Cupidon for long, green pods, Safari for cropping thin, long beans over a long period, and Sonesta or Orinoco for waxy, yellow pods.

Purple Tepee grows flavoursome beans that appear to go from too small to too large in as little as 3 days, but do not appear to be tough or stringy.